The Wedding Dress Survival Guide

A humorous, no-bullshit guide to help you say "Yes" without the stress!

Siân Leyshon-Fleming

The Wedding Dress Survival Guide
A humorous, no-bullshit guide to help you say "Yes" without the stress!

ISBN: 9781068331602 Paperback

Published by: Inspired By Publishing

Dedication

I am dedicating this book to the thousands of brides I have met over the past 10 years.

The ones that make me fall in love with my job over and over again and the ones who make me want to jump off a bridge…over and over again.

Without you, there would be no book.

Oh, and I also need to dedicate this to my beautiful son, Hector. You are, without a doubt, my greatest achievement.

Dammit, I need to mention my gorgeous hubby, Adam. The fog lifted when you came into view...

…and my dogs…I can't forget my dogs, can I?

Foreword

In my opinion, there is no one better than Sian to write a book like this one. She brings together an impressive career with authenticity, honesty and a brilliant sense of humour. Her extensive experience allows her to understand the intricacies of dresses whilst her hilarious, no-bullshit approach makes the often daunting task of wedding dress shopping feel accessible and most importantly, fun!

I know that for Sian, this is one of the most rewarding parts of her work. It's a reminder that the path to finding the perfect gown isn't just about ticking boxes, it is about breaking free from preconceived notions about what the bride *should* wear and instead celebrating their individuality.

Every bride must read this book because it really is one of a kind! I don't know of any other guide for brides that offers a refreshing combination of humour and knowledge with no-nonsense, practical advice from an industry expert who tailors advice and solutions to the unique challenges brides face.

It's not just a manual for finding a wedding dress, it's a down-to-earth, relatable guide that reassures brides that it's okay to feel overwhelmed. With Sian's candid, no-holds-barred approach and relatable anecdotes, she demystifies the process and empowers brides to embrace the chaos rather than fear it. Sian has witnessed thousands of fittings, shared in countless moments of joy and even navigated the occasional drama.

What I love about this book is its authenticity. Sian doesn't sugarcoat the experience – she dives headfirst into the moments that make you laugh, cry and sometimes question your sanity. She understands that a wedding dress isn't just about the fabric, it's about how you *feel* when you wear it. It's about the stories you'll share and the memories you'll create. This deep understanding of a bride's emotional ups and downs allows Sian to provide invaluable insights and relatable anecdotes that will resonate with anyone stepping into a bridal shop.

So whether you're just starting your shopping journey or are deep into your fittings, with Sian's guidance, you'll not only find the perfect wedding gown but also *enjoy* the journey – transforming what can be a nerve-wracking experience into a fun and memorable adventure.

Enjoy all the laughs that are waiting for you in the pages ahead!

Charlie Brear

Charlie Brear is a renowned British bridal and fashion designer. Charlie's label is known for its innovative approach to bridal and eveningwear, incorporating vintage elements and contemporary designs. Dressing celebrities in both the UK and the USA on the red carpet, the CB brand is stocked in boutiques worldwide. Her success as a designer has earned her recognition in the fashion industry, with features in prestigious publications such as Vogue, Tatler and Harper's Bazaar and write-ups by BOF, WWD & The Wall Street Journal.

Contents

Contents

Introduction

You're engaged! Yay to you! And while that stunning solitaire engagement ring is what you've been waiting for, let's be honest, there's one part of wedding planning that fills you with either excitement or terror: Dress shopping! And I'm here to guide you through it.

Your wedding dress is more than just a piece of fabric, it's an expression of your personality, an expression you will wear on one of the biggest days of your life. You are about to go on an exciting journey – one that can quickly turn into one bloody big palaver if you aren't armed and ready. That's where this guide comes in. Welcome to the insane world of wedding dresses!

In this no-holds-barred guide, we'll navigate your journey to finding that one dress that makes you feel like the magnificent human being you are. From appointment preparation to the first time you enter a bridal shop, all the way to your final alterations, I'll help you tackle them all with a clear head and zero need for anti-stress herbal supplements.

Now is the perfect time for you to dive into my guide to dress shopping. As the wedding planning progresses, so does the pressure. With so many decisions to make, I don't blame you for feeling overwhelmed. By embracing the comedy and madness of wedding dress shopping, you'll not only relieve the pressure on yourself, but you'll also have some newly acquired knowledge that will give you the confidence to tackle those fitting rooms like a pro.

So, what's so different about this book compared to all the other wedding and bridal tomes available these days? Well for a start, everything I share is based on my first-hand experience…as a bride (twice) and as an experienced bridal boutique owner. This means I'm not here to fill your brains with old wives' tales, weird bridal jargon and impractical advice about how to find your dream wedding dress. I'm here to cut through all that bullshit. I'm here to help.

Why did I feel the need to create a guide like the one you have in your hands? My experience as a newly engaged thirty-something was, well, beige. I have always worked in the luxury goods industry and by the time I started my dress-shopping journey in 2011, I was working for a famous British fashion designer. You could say my expectations were perhaps slightly higher than most others.

However, I honestly felt that the basics weren't even present at any of my appointments. There was no advice, no guidance…There just wasn't an experience. Don't get me wrong, most of the people I met were lovely, but it made me realise that I had an opportunity to provide brides with a service that was knowledgeable and authentic in a luxe, relaxed, yet fun environment. I could provide them with an *experience*. So, in 2014 I opened my bridal store Tilly Trotter's Brides.

Fast forward to 2025 and the number of bridal boutiques in the UK alone has increased significantly. This means the variety and choice for brides have also significantly increased, along with a bride's expectation of boutiques. Consequently, brides are struggling to find their way amidst the chaotic world of wedding dresses, and boutiques are struggling to compete with each other and meet the ever-increasing demands of brides. To be honest it's just getting a bit too much for all of us.

I am here to give you a no-bullshit guide to dress shopping. Considering the fact that you are reading this introduction, I'm guessing that wedding planning is already driving you crazy and the pressure of finding the "perfect" wedding dress is just the final straw. Am I right?

Well, breathe a sigh of relief, my love, as I am here to drown out all of that background noise and help you hear and listen to your instincts, so that when you do find the wedding dress of your dreams you will know that it's not been forced. It's not a decision you've made under pressure. You've found it because you felt it in the pit of your belly, that feeling that you were "home" in a wedding gown meant for *you*.

Whether your vision is chic Hollywood glamour or vintage fairytale, I will arm you with the survival skills you need to tackle everything from unsolicited opinions to dress sizes that seem to have their own sick agenda.

As we embark on this hilariously crazy journey together, let me share a few of my personal beliefs that guide my approach to wedding dress shopping. First, and most importantly, I firmly believe that your perfect wedding dress should not only make you look spectacular but also make you feel like *you*. I know it's a bit of a cringey cliché, but your mission should be to look like a better version of yourself. It's about embracing your own style and personality and not conforming to anyone else's preconceived ideas or expectations of what you as a bride "should" look like.

Secondly, please remember that this whole experience is about you and your love story. A wedding dress should celebrate who you are, quirks and all.

With this in mind, I encourage you to release all of the pressure (we can burn some sage and bathe in the power of the moonlight if that helps. You do you), embrace the absurdity, and dive headfirst into this adventure.

Brace yourself, bridey! It's time to embrace the chaotic world of bridal and find the wedding dress of your dreams amid the madness.

Sian (aka Tilly)

-XOXO-

Chapter 1
"Shit Just Got Real!"

Marriage is an adventure. Like going to war.

OMG, YAS! You're engaged! Congratulations!

Isn't it the best feeling ever? That little bubble of love that makes the stars seem brighter, the sun sunnier, the flowers more…flowery.

Enjoy the moment, even just for a few weeks. Soak it up. Gratefully receive the love and happiness everyone wants to shower on you. While this may be the most exciting time of your life, I promise you the novelty will wear off pretty quickly for your nearest and dearest… and they'll lose interest within a few weeks. Losers.

If you are anything like the bride I was (the first time around!) wedding planning will now take over your life, and you'll want to discuss those Pinterest mood boards in *great* detail with just about anyone who will listen. The only problem is that no one actually wants to listen anymore because you used up all of your "Interested Bridesmaid" vouchers within the first month of being engaged.

But don't worry, that's what I am here for! Your friendly bridal boutique owner, serial bride and wedding dress fairy godmother.

I'm here to help take you through one part of the wedding planning process – your search for *the dress* – and make it as seamless, relaxed and *fun* as shopping should be. And let's face it, it really is the *most* important part of any wedding. I'm not interested in all that waffle about marrying the love of your life etc. Ultimately, you need to look like a goddess and people need to be talking about your incredible bridal style until the end of time. This book will guide you through your dress shopping journey from booking your bridal boutique appointments to the pros and cons of nipple covers, with a few "real-life bride" stories along the way.

So balls to all those idiots who don't want to sit for hours and discuss the difference between fishtail and mermaid wedding dresses! I'll hold your hand and we can chat about it for hours.

I *totally* appreciate how important this dress is. Whether you are the bride who has been planning her wedding since she was nine years old or the bride who has never given her future wedding a moment's thought. Both of you will have a "version" in your minds of what dress shopping will and should look like. You are about to have an experience that will remain in your memory boxes forever.

So where do you even begin with wedding gown shopping? Particularly when there are so many bloody shops to choose from?

When I was an Area Manager in my previous life, I used to drive past the same bridal shop every week and I always told myself that's where I would go to find my dream dress when I got engaged. I loved the shopfront, I loved their window displays and I *loved* the dresses. So when I finally did get proposed to, I booked an appointment and trotted off to the aforementioned boutique, ready to find the dress of my dreams.

I'd been lusting over designer Jenny Packham for years and adored her gowns; the intricate beadwork, the achingly beautiful embroidery, the *everything*. And there was no doubt in my mind that I would be wearing one of Jenny's designs on my wedding day.

It's worth mentioning here that I wasn't working in the bridal industry at this point in my life, and although I worked in luxury fashion, I soon found out that bridal is a whole different ball game.

However! My expectations were pretty much shot to shit before I'd even made it over the boutique's threshold. All I saw when I entered was a sea, no, an *ocean*, of wedding dresses and two snotty women analysing me from behind the desk.

Now, I'm not easily intimidated, but I could feel my cheeks flushing. I had to suppress the uncontrollable urge to sprint over and shove my engagement ring in the women's faces, yelling

"Look! I'm engaged! I promise I do belong here! Please accept me as one of your own!"

Obviously, I'm a little more restrained than that. So I just acted as my usual, over-confident self, threw out one of my comic one-liners (I can't remember what exactly, but I'm sure it was hysterical) and lay myself at the mercy of these pretentious, but highly experienced and knowledgeable (surely?) bitches.

Unfortunately, the snotty bitches (let's call them the "SBs") had other plans.

Zero interest was shown in my engagement ring or my wedding plans (could they not tell that this was all I wanted to talk about every single minute of every single day?), let alone the dress I'd been dreaming of since forever. Instead, the SBs handed me some plastic discs, you know, like the ones you're given in the H&M fitting rooms, and told me to look through the dresses and put a disc on the hanger of any dress I wanted to try.

Thanks, SBs. That's really helpful of you.

Anyway, aided by the power of my magical plastic discs, I selected some Jenny Packham dresses to try and followed the Chief SB into the fitting room to disrobe.

Alarm bell number two: Have you ever undressed in front of a complete stranger whilst said stranger is just standing there staring at you? In silence!? Those of you who know me personally will know that I am certainly not shy and will, after a few strawberry daiquiris, happily get my boobs out for any interested party. However, this was different. This was just weird and extremely uncomfortable. I had to stand there in my underwear whilst the SB unzipped the gown and laid it out on the floor for me to step into. Again, in silence. (Perhaps she was mute? I should've asked Deputy SB).

And, well, long story short…I looked like a sausage.

I needed to be tall, slim and waif-like to pull off these whimsical beauties, all of which I absolutely was not.

Nevertheless, I pulled up my big girl knickers and waited with anticipation for the SBs to put a reassuring hand on my shoulder and guide me toward some alternative dresses that would hopefully make me look less like a meat-based product and more like the bridal beauty I had dreamt of.

Alas! The reassuring hand did not appear and so I was left to my own devices, aimlessly wandering around the store and selecting some more dresses to try, none of which suited me, all of which made me feel like the size of a sperm whale.

So I gave up, left the boutique and went to a nearby pub to get myself blind drunk.

With my sob story in mind, let's look at what makes a good bridal boutique and how to spot the lesser-known species amongst a herd of below-average stores.

How to Choose Your Bridal Boutique

Reviews or Word of Mouth

A recommended bridal boutique is, in my opinion, the most important factor to consider when sifting through the masses. It doesn't matter how many Instagram ads a boutique rams down your throat. If they don't have a wonderful reputation for the impeccable care of their brides, then I wouldn't touch them with a barge pole.

Take time to not only look at the quantity of high-rated reviews they have but also the *content*. What are the reviewers actually saying about their experiences?

For example, my boutique has over one hundred 5-star reviews, but the overall rating dropped to 4.9 due to a MOB (mother of the bride – I won't tell you her name, but it rhymes with "Natricia") giving us a 3-star rating because the hanger provided with her daughter's dress "didn't meet her expectations"! (Apparently, she was expecting a gold-plated clothes hanger).

Designers

Another important one. I really don't see the point of visiting a boutique if you haven't checked to see if you actually like the bridal designers they stock.

I'm not suggesting that you need to know at this stage if the dresses they hold will *suit* you. That will come later on during your appointment. But if you're looking at the images on a shop's website and are physically repulsed by what you see, then there's a high chance you won't like them a significant amount more when you see them in person.

You also don't want to find yourself in a situation wherein you arrive at a boutique only to find that they stock 356,792 bridal designers, but they all look exactly the same. A shop that celebrates its vast stock directory does not necessarily mean that it will be able to offer you a varied choice of dress styles. Many boutiques hold a number of designers that all produce the same style of gown, which is just confusing for any bride.

Less is more. Too many choices are just confusing.

If you can find a shop that carries multiple dress designers and dress styles, then you will minimise the feeling of the need to shop elsewhere.

I would recommend doing some research before you start booking appointments. Hit up the usual suspects, like Pinterest and Instagram, to see if there are any dresses that catch your eye, then take note of the style and designer. You could even take it a step further and search hashtags of the specific dress style to see some images of real brides wearing that designer's dresses. It's always more helpful to see a realistic picture of a bride as opposed to an airbrushed supermodel.

It's also worth checking out some wedding blogs such as (my personal fave) www.rockmywedding.co.uk where you'll find some amazing wedding inspo – not just dresses, but venues, flowers, photographers and so on.

Experience

How long have they been trading for? How experienced are the staff?

Boutiques don't need to have been open for donkey's years to be considered a "good" store. However, I would expect the owner or stylists of a newly opened boutique to at least have some previous experience in the industry or to have taken the time to undergo some training to understand the intricacies of bridal wear. They need to be able to understand the construction of a wedding gown, the varying fabrics, the different cuts of a dress and so on. Otherwise, how will they be able to confidently recommend suitable dress shapes and styles for all of our different body types?

Likewise, are the stylists taking time to sit down and learn about your wedding, your personal style, what you love, what you hate?

Are you having a casual beach wedding? Or is it going to be a more formal or romantic affair? For my team, all of this information plays a vital role in the dresses we recommend to our brides. So I truly feel that if a consultant isn't taking the time to ask questions like these, you should question their authenticity.

Tip! If you are struggling to verbalise the elements of wedding dresses that you like and dislike, then I suggest trying to come up with two or three adjectives that would describe your dream dress. Those two little words can tell a bridal stylist everything they need to know!

"Reflecting on my bridal shopping experience, I realised that the key difference was the approach of the person helping me. It wasn't just about finding a dress, it was about finding someone who was willing to invest the time to understand me and had the expertise to guide me, even if it meant challenging my expectations."

– Real bride, Lily

Website

Is the website inviting and easy to navigate? If it's so fancy that you can't even make it past a boutique's digital front door, then chances are the store itself won't be particularly warm and accessible.

Is the website content up to date? When I was beginning my dress search for Husband Number 1, I spotted a dress in a bridal magazine that I became obsessed with and was desperate to try. After a painstaking Google search I finally found one UK stockist that held the designer and, according to their website, that exact dress.

However, when I called them to book an appointment specifically to try that particular dress, the staff had no idea what I was talking about! They didn't know the designer and had no recollection of having that gown in the boutique. Turns out the boutique had stopped stocking my sought-after designer months ago, they just forgot to update their website.

And here endeth my lesson.

"I was very nervous prior to the appointment as I'm not a very confident person so I knew I only wanted to go to one shop because I knew I would end up feeling really overwhelmed. The boutique I chose told me everything I needed to know on its website. They had such a great selection of dresses on there to look through so I got a great idea about what to expect before my appointment.

My research showed me that all bridal shops have the same style of wedding dresses, so for me it was about picking the "right" shop to book an appointment for. Ultimately, I wanted the experience to be easy, fun and exciting!"

– Real bride, Abbie

Outlet Stores and Sample Sales

Now don't be a snob about these! They may not be your conventional, run-of-the-mill bridal store, but if you have a limited budget or are working on a very short lead time, then these bridal outlets and bridal sample sales are incredible!

They generally stock ex-samples, which means they are likely to be gowns that have been tried on by previous brides and possibly show some signs of wear, but you'll be able to take it home with you on the day and not be subjected to the long production lead times (more on that later) and for a *significantly* reduced price. For example, at my boutique's most recent sample sale, I featured a gown by highly sought-after, uber-luxe designer Galia Lahav that retailed for over £8,000, and I sold it to a delighted bride for £2,500! The bride was over the moon as she was able to wear a gown by a designer that was previously way out of her budget. I was over the moon as I was able to rehome a dress that was discontinued and consequently, there was no reason for me to keep in store.

Please don't feel like you are compromising by visiting an outlet or sample sale. They've come a huge way since the days of that *Friends* episode, where it's every man for themselves and Rachel has to hide behind a garment rail fearfully blowing her whistle! You'll find that many off-the-peg stores are identical to a "normal" boutique in both interior design and service. A perfect example of an amazing store is Off The Peg by Dotty (www.offthepegbridal. co.uk) where you can find fantastic ex-sample gowns, housed in a beautiful store and looked after by a warm, friendly and highly trained team.

No compromising here!

Trunkshows

Bridal boutiques rarely hold an entire collection from one designer, and you will typically find an edited collection that the team has curated with *their* brides in mind. So if a store advertises that they are hosting a trunkshow, it means they will have an entire collection from one specific designer, usually for a very limited period of time. This is a particularly great event to attend if it involves the collections of a designer that you love.

As an added bonus, some boutiques offer a discount during this event, so you may even get the chance to save a bit of cash too!

Before Setting an Appointment

Set the Date

This book isn't a wedding planner so I'm not about to talk you through the next steps to take in order to pull off the celebration of the century. However, there is one thing you need to get sorted before you even start thinking about dress shopping…

Book. Your. Venue.

It won't be the first time you'll hear me say this, but please don't dress for your venue. I truly believe that you should wear exactly what you want to wear and not something that suits where you're getting married. However, you do need to have a date for your wedding. Unless you plan to purchase your dress from an outlet, you will be at the mercy of a designer's lead times, which can be anything from six months to a year. If you set your wedding date for a day in August but don't actually start your dress search until a few weeks (or even a couple of months!) before, then it's highly unlikely that any shop will be able to order you a dress that will be made and then altered in time for your wedding.

I'll go into more detail about your alterations later on.

You also need to bear in mind that your dress is *made to order* (made to a standard dress size) and it is very likely it will need further alterations once it has been delivered. It is advised that you allow around eight weeks after your dress has been delivered to enable your seamstress to comfortably schedule all of your fittings in time for your wedding.

Finally, please be aware that if you don't allow enough time to order your dress, you may be faced with rush order fees, which can sometimes be as much as an additional 30% of the price of your dress.

But don't shop too early! If you are planning on a long engagement and start shopping for a dress immediately, you run the risk of your dress going out of style. Or even worse, being discontinued.

Dresses regularly get discontinued and this can be for a number of reasons, but it is usually because either the designer is retiring the style or there is an element of the dress – the lace for example – that they are unable to source any longer. This discontinuation is typically effective immediately and with no prior notice. Believe me when I tell you this happens more often than you think!

So the point I'm trying to emphasise here is if you find your dream wedding dress (and if you follow my guidance in this book, I promise you that you will!) then please just order it. It's really not worth the risk of not being able to have it.

Organise Your Entourage

I totally get it. This is a bloody important decision. This is likely to be the most photographed dress you will ever own. So if you know that you are an indecisive person who cannot possibly commit to a dress without having your mum, bridesmaids, aunt, favourite primary school teacher, the lady who works at Sainsbury's with you, then don't book an appointment until you have agreed on a date that everyone can attend. See my previous point about the likelihood of finding your dream dress at your first appointment. You don't want that magical moment ruined because you don't have all of your favourite cheerleaders with you.

Worst case scenario: If it's impossible to get everyone together (and in my opinion, if someone bails on your wedding dress appointment then you should, quite simply, cut them out of your life) then ask the shop to help you video call them so they can still be involved and your moment isn't ruined.

Whilst we are on the subject of your entourage, make sure you choose wisely. It's great to have all of your gang with you. But if we're honest, they don't always have the bride's interests at heart and can often get distracted by dresses *they* love rather than dresses they love the *bride* in.

I've also found that girls can sometimes just be a bit bloody mean to each other! I have met numerous sulky sisters who are simply downright jealous of the bride and (whether they realise they're doing it or not) seem to want to do or say anything they can to ruin the whole dress-shopping experience.

It is worth having a chat with your gang whilst you're making your way over to your bridal appointment. Just to, you know, *manage* their expectations! Set boundaries with them and let them know what you are looking for when it comes to feedback.

Let them know how important their opinions are and how you have included them in this appointment as you value them so much. It is important that they know they can be honest, but they need to be *kind*. However, ultimately this is going to be *your* decision and they need to allow you to choose a dress that *you* love, regardless of their thoughts and opinions.

Tip! One of my brides asked her team to not say anything until she had come out of the fitting room and properly looked at herself in the mirror. This worked a treat, as it meant that the bride could genuinely take on board her mum and bridesmaid's opinions after she had made her own.

One last point on entourage: Too many cooks can definitely spoil the bridal broth. It may seem like a fun idea to take 84 people shopping with you, but the novelty will definitely wear off once everyone is throwing their opinions out and confusing the hell out of you. Moreover, too many opinions can make you feel less sure about your decision.

It's Perfectly Fine to Shop Alone

I don't want to harp on about having an entourage to bring with you if you intend to shop for your dress alone. It is totally normal to visit your bridal boutique without a gang of bridesmaids so please don't let anyone tell you otherwise.

Shopping for your dress alone with just your bridal consultant to aid you means that you will be making a decision with a clear head, void of any other opinions and external influences.

Choose ONE Boutique

Assuming you've done some homework and managed to find a few designers that you love, get yourself onto Google and find a store that stocks as many of your faves as you can.

Now, this is controversial and may be difficult for you, but I honestly think the best way to start your dress journey is to just make *one* appointment. By all means, make a shortlist of a few boutiques that you'd ideally like to visit, but just select the one that is at the top of your list to visit first.

There is an extremely high chance that you could find your dress at your first appointment and it would be really sad if you ruin that amazing moment simply because you have one, two, three more shops to visit.

As someone who has been married twice, believe me when I tell you that you'll find your dream dress when you least expect it. And in my opinion, when you're taken by surprise it's the best possible situation to be in because you know that you've found The One. It's not forced.

So don't ruin the moment. Book one appointment, and if you don't find your dress at your first shop then go ahead and book the next one on your shortlist.

"The idea of wedding dress shopping felt daunting to me. Unlike the excitement you often see on TV, I didn't feel thrilled about the experience. I booked my first bridal appointment with mixed feelings. The first store I visited had dresses off the rack, and they didn't allow photos, which made me feel uneasy right away. With no clear idea of what I wanted, I ended up trying on nearly everything, but nothing caught my eye.

At the second shop, I felt overwhelmed again. I tried on about 12 dresses, and it seemed like I was starting to narrow down my preferences to a fitted, sleek and simple style. However, none of the dresses felt quite right, and I left feeling uncertain."

– Real bride, Lily

Know Your Budget

Let me set the record straight: You don't need to spend a fortune to find a stunning wedding dress. One of the designers I stock creates the most beautifully made gowns (incredible corsetry, exquisite fabrics) and retails at an average of £1,700. Believe me, that really isn't a huge amount to invest to get such a beautiful gown.

Regardless of how much you want to spend on your dress (and I'm not talking about the amount you have *budgeted* for your dress, I'm talking about the amount you realistically want to *spend)* all I ask is that you be honest with your bridal boutique. There is absolutely no point in telling your stylist that you have a £3,000 budget when you actually have no intention of spending more than £2,000 on your dress. You will just end up wasting precious appointment time trying on dresses that are over budget, when you can use that time to try more gowns that are in your price range and thus, have more to choose from.

Likewise, please don't book an appointment at a boutique if you know that the dresses they stock are out of your price range, because I guarantee that you *will* find a dress that you absolutely love and then you'll just leave there feeling miserable and hating life. There's no point doing that to yourself when there are so many dresses available out there within your budget.

You'll also really piss the boutique off if you take up a one to two-hour appointment when you have no intention of getting a dress from there. I know it's harsh, but I need to say it.

So please don't be *that* bride.

Be Prepared to Say "Yes!"

It may sound obvious, but there's no point in starting shopping if you have no intention of saying "yes to the dress" when you find it!

Bridal Know-How

Use this pre-shopping checklist before you book a boutique:

- You have set your wedding date.

- You've organised your Bride Tribe to make sure all the VIPs will be able to attend your appointment with you.

- You know what your dress budget is and how much you are prepared to spend on it.

- You have researched your dress shop and are clear on the price range of the dresses they stock.

- You are ready to say yes to the dress if you find it!

If you are still feeling a bit vague on some of the information you've gathered about your bridal boutique, here are some questions you may want to consider asking before booking your appointment:

- What is the price range of your dresses?

- Are all the gowns you have shown on your website?

- If you don't have a specific gown in store are you able to request to borrow it from the designer? Is there an additional charge for this?

- Will my wedding date affect the lead time of my dress?

- What size are your samples?

- Will you require a deposit to order my dress? If so, how much?

- Do you have an in-house seamstress? If not, can you recommend one?

- What is the average cost of alterations?

So let's get that appointment booked and start shopping!

Chapter 2
"When Do We Get Champagne?"

Marriage lets you annoy the same person for the rest of your life.

Fabulous! You've listened to my advice and booked your appointment at *one* bridal boutique (insert wry smile emoji!). Let's get this dress-shopping party on the road!

In this chapter, I want to reiterate the importance of researching your bridal shops before booking an appointment and share with you the disastrous results of "expectations versus reality." If you attend your first bridal appointment unarmed with important information, then you will undoubtedly leave feeling deflated and overwhelmed.

Assuming you've done your homework, then you've found a boutique that stocks some or all the dress designers you've been coveting, has fabulous reviews, testimonials and experienced stylists *and* offers a fantastic, celebratory shopping experience. If the store ticks all the boxes, then we're definitely heading off on the right path.

However, even though we've done all the groundwork on the shop selection, we really must do a little groundwork on ourselves.

Brideys, it's time to manage your expectations....

The Experience

As I said, whether you are the sort of person who has been planning their wedding since being in the womb with a detailed scrapbook of ideas to complement, or you are the person who hasn't given weddings a moment's thought as you've been spending your informative years paving the way as an independent w.o.m.a.n, you will still have an expectation as to what wedding dress shopping should and will look like.

You've seen the films, you've read the books, you've heard the stories. You are expecting to enter a boutique with an uber-luxe interior, to be serenaded by a carefully curated Spotify playlist, to have the delicate scent of aromatherapy candles kiss your little nostrils whilst you recline on a chaise longue and sip champagne. All the while having bridal stylists sit and attentively listen to all of your wedding dress hopes and dreams...

And I hope you get an experience like the one you've dreamt of. I really, really do. However, the media has a lot to answer for and I have to mention the dreaded show, *Say Yes To The Dress*.

Now don't get me wrong. This TV show is as much a guilty pleasure for me as it is for you. But let me set the record straight: That programme is not accurate. I know several brides who were featured in the UK version of that show (some of whom actually came to my own boutique to order their dream dress after having their "*SYTTD* appointment," which says a LOT!). I can honestly tell you that not only is that TV show highly produced and intrinsically choreographed, but the brides and their guests go through a rigorous casting process to ensure they will provide as much entertainment as possible for the audience's viewing pleasure. Believe me, whether that entertainment consists of 236 bridesmaids critiquing each wedding gown and ripping a bride's self-confidence to shreds with their opinions, or a bride bursting into hysterical tears of joy because she's found *the* dress, they'll be sure to have all that on camera for people to watch (myself included!).

The latter is unrealistic and rarely happens and the former is just plain bitchy. Who wants bridesmaids like that?

It's quite rare to find a bridal boutique the size of an airport hanger, so if you're worrying about being overwhelmed with choice, there's no need. Moreover, if *SYTTD* has terrified you into thinking that your entourage is going to annihilate you with negative opinions as soon as you step out of the fitting room, then please don't panic. I'd like to think that you aren't actually going to have total bitches as friends or bridesmaids. And if they do start acting a little overzealous with their feedback on how you look, then politely tell them to fuck off.

It's also worth highlighting that walking into a bridal shop that stocks as many dresses as US store Kleinfeld isn't necessarily a good thing. You might remember the tale of my first bridal shopping experience, where I was greeted by hundreds of wedding dresses and had absolutely no idea where to start. It certainly didn't help that those SBs had zero interest in helping me. I was already overwhelmed by the sheer number of choices, and the actual fitting part only made it worse (and it isn't just because of the silent SB who watched me undress!).

Sample Sizes

When I finally did get dresses I wanted to try on during my fateful first visit to a bridal boutique, I couldn't squeeze my generously sized backside into the majority of them and the ones that I could get into would definitely not zip up. I felt like the Marshmallow Man from the *Ghostbusters* films. If you try your usual size and end up looking like a fellow Marshmallow Man, know that it happens. Let me introduce you to the magic (or curse?) that is bridal sizing.

First, note that bridal sizing differs from designer to designer. Just because a size 12 wedding dress fits you in one designer's collection, doesn't mean a size 12 will fit in another. Second, bridal clothing generally comes up smaller in comparison to your typical high street shopping and your dress, when ordered, will likely be one to two sizes higher than you would normally wear.

Finally, know that it's highly unlikely you'll be able to zip up a dress and trot out of the fitting room with a gown that fits like a glove. This is because most of us are split between two or three sizes (for example, I have a size 12 bust measurement and a size 14 hip), but dresses are made to one standard size.

To be fair to the bridal boutique, I didn't actually research what sizes the dresses would be before I attended my appointment. However, it would have been helpful (and far less humiliating) if the shop contacted me beforehand or even explained to me at the start of my appointment the difference between high street sizing and bridal, and where their shop samples sit in comparison. Had I known that this particular boutique only stocked samples in sizes UK 8 and 10, I would have avoided them in the same way I avoid gyms – like the plague. A truly fabulous boutique should be able to use its skills and expertise to pin or clip you in almost any size sample dress, be it too big or too small. It won't be perfect, but it should at least be able to give you a good idea of how the dress will look when it's ordered in a more appropriate size.

Be Open-Minded

Pretty much all of my brides end up ordering a dress that is nothing like what they thought they would have, a dress like those on their Pinterest board or a dress that is the same as the one that they came to their appointment wanting to try.

It's great to have a wish list and some styles of dresses in mind before your appointment, but please be open-minded to the likelihood that all of this will go out of the window when you actually get the dresses on your body. If you're not in this mindset then you're really going to struggle to find a dress that's perfect for you.

You could also have a nosey at some real brides' photographs and celeb weddings and see if any styles resonate with you.

A great boutique will recommend some styles that are the same as those on your vision board, but will also recommend alternatives that, in their experience, will suit you better.

Ultimately, the stylist's goal should be to make you look and feel the absolute goddess that you are…the best you've ever looked. Anything less than that is simply unacceptable. Now that I own a successful bridal boutique, I look back at this gross experience and simply ensure that my team and I are doing the complete opposite!

But what does that look like to you lovely brides?

From my perspective, the ideal wedding dress shop should provide the following:

- Someone to greet you when you arrive and not make you feel like a dick for being there.

- Your own personal stylist who takes the time to ask questions about you and your wedding and *listens* to your answers.

- The chance to peruse the dresses and select some you love, but also have consultants that can make recommendations they know will suit your vision, style and body shape.

- Stylists and attendants who are able to confidently offer alternatives to dresses that aren't working for you.

If none of this is happening, then run, girl, *run away.*

"I was dreading the dress shopping process and having (unsuccessfully) already visited other stores, I was starting to worry that I wouldn't ever find the perfect dress. As I glanced around the shop, I didn't see anything in the style I thought I liked, but then the stylist took the time to sit with me and get to know me. None of the other shops had done this. Her genuine interest helped me relax, even as she began pulling out dresses I had specifically said I didn't want – strapless or full-skirted gowns. She insisted I try on a particular dress she had in mind, despite my scepticism.

To my surprise, when I put these wild cards on, I felt a spark of excitement. It was comfortable, and there was something very special about it. I continued trying on other dresses, but none of them compared to that first one, even though it was completely different from what I thought I wanted. In the end, I chose the strapless, full-skirted gown – the very style I initially rejected – because the bridal consultant truly knew her craft. She took the time to understand me and had the confidence to say, 'Trust me, I know what I'm doing.'"

— Real bride, Lily

I know this is a lot to take in and we haven't even got to the good bit (trying on the dresses!) yet. So below is a little summary of all the important bits.

Chapter Takeaways

Manage your expectations. Reality TV is not real life and if you pay too much attention to it, you'll either end up too scared to book an appointment or bitterly disappointed with the reality.

If you're body conscious, contact your chosen boutique before your appointment (either give them a call or trawl through the FAQs on their website) and ask them to confirm the sizes of dresses that they have in their store

Be open-minded and prepared to walk away from your appointment with a dress that is nothing like the one you envisaged. You want simple, fitted and understated? I guarantee that you'll leave the boutique having ordered the biggest, sparkliest ballgown you've ever seen!

You can do this, bridey! Now let's get those dresses on you!

Chapter 3
"Get That Bloody Dress on Me Immediately!"

Turns out, I love you more than I originally anticipated.

The day has finally arrived! You've rounded up your absolute best cheerleaders, you've loaded up your credit card and you've spent the last month or so sucking up to your mum so that she doesn't kick off if you go over your dress budget. You've even selected your most bridal style of outfit, one that says "I'm a very demure and elegant bride-to-be, but also it's *my* fucking day and don't any of you forget that."

Feeling a bit anxious or nervous? Don't worry, that's completely normal! In this chapter I'm going to ease you into your dress appointment and talk you through everything that happens at the start of your shopping experience, focusing on wedding dress shapes, styles and what to expect when you finally get those stunning gowns onto your stunning bodies.

I'm hoping that by the end of this chapter, you will have filled your arsenal with loads of helpful info so that you can go into your dress appointment feeling giddy with excitement, not giddy with nerves!

Selecting Which Dresses to Try

As I mentioned earlier on in this book, the right bridal stylist will start your appointment by sitting down with you and asking all about your wedding. What's your wedding vibe? Rustic and boho? Understated elegance? Small and intimate? Cathedral grandeur? Black-tie glamour? Whatever style of wedding you're going for, providing your stylists with all the deets will help them to start creating a "mood board" in their mind of the sort of dresses that may compliment your vision.

Moving on to you, The Bride. What sort of wedding dresses have you been drawn towards? What's on your Pinterest board? Is there anything you particularly love? Anything you especially hate? What's the most important thing about your dress? Do we need to factor in the logistics of flying around the dance floor to a Ceilidh band?

All of this information will help your stylist collate a list of gowns for you to try that not only tick all of your boxes but also include some "wild cards," a couple of dresses that you would never, in a million years, consider trying on. You should definitely trust your stylist in this instance. They know their collections inside and out and will be pulling these wild cards based on that knowledge and their confidence that these dresses will look banging on you! So be open to trying all the different styles of dresses your stylist recommends. It's the old adage – wedding dresses really do look completely different when a bride is wearing them compared to when they're hanging on the rails.

I personally believe that a bride shouldn't be limited to how many dresses she is allowed to try on. However, I know that some boutiques do try and encourage brides to only select a specific amount to prevent the bride from becoming overwhelmed, which I completely appreciate and am totally on board with.

Regardless of whether you are limited or not, it's worth bearing in mind that, in my experience, brides typically try on around 8 to 10 dresses before settling on The One.

One more note on choosing dresses: Please try and have a gentle word with your entourage before you arrive at your boutique about crowd control. I *know* how exciting wedding dress shopping is (like, I *really* know…I've done it twice!), and the idea of getting all of your guests to choose a "fun" or "alternative" dress for you to try (usually just for the crack – they're rarely helpful suggestions) is just a pain in the arse for bridal stylists. Your friends and family won't know the collections as well as the bridal shop and ultimately it's just going to eat into your appointment and limit the time you'll have to try on the dresses that truly suit you, your shape and your style of wedding.

I would also like to take this chance to say that you can and should consider non-white dresses. Pure white dresses aren't as common as they used to be and this is because there are so many different variations of ivory that are available (like bright ivory, subtle eggshell etc). Ivory also varies from designer to designer and fabric to fabric. For example, an ivory dress made in mikado within one designer's collection can look completely different from that of another designer.

Many designers (such as Madi Lane Bridal) also offer brides the option of having their dress made in a different colour or tone which is always worth considering if the option is presented to you. Take an ivory dress and change the lining to a romantic blush and it can go from a 7/10 to a 10/10.

Don't be afraid to be different!

Here are the different types of silhouettes and necklines you might come across. Keep these handy in your vocab during your dress shopping!

The Important Stuff

A-Line and a Soft A-Line

So called because the shape pretty much resembles a capital "A." It is fitted at the bodice (the smaller bit of the A) and then gradually becomes fuller in the skirt (the wider part of the A).

This A-line dress has a sweetheart neckline which works particularly well on fuller busts as it draws attention to your gorgeous decolletage and makes your neck appear longer.

The square neckline on this soft A-line dress also suits pretty much everyone. It's particularly great for balancing out a silhouette by drawing attention to the top half of the body.

The Soft A-Line is simply, as in the name, a softer, floatier version of an A-Line!

Great for: This shape is universally flattering and compliments all body types. However, it looks particularly great on us curvier, pear-shaped girls because it defines the waist area and floats over the hips.

Avoid if: If nothing! It suits all of us.

Ballgown

When you think of a ballgown, this style of dress immediately springs to mind, no? I like to describe it as an A-Line dress with a caffeine shot! It has the same fitted bodice to accentuate your waist, but the skirt is mega princessy and glamorous.

Great for: Those of you (sadly, not I) who are blessed with big boobs or if you feel like you have slightly broad shoulders as the fuller skirt balances everything out!

Avoid if: You are a petite bride. The dress will swallow you up and we won't be able to find you amongst all that fabric!

Get the full Princess vibe with a sweetheart neckline and a ballgown skirt.

This is another variation with a square neckline and thinner straps.

Basque

This shape really is the trend of the season! It has a fitted bodice that finishes just past the natural waistline (often to a point giving the shape of a "V").

Great for: If you have a short body, this is perfect for you as it elongates the torso.

Avoid if: You're like me and have a little paunch or food baby belly that you'd prefer to disguise as it defines the waist and can draw attention to that area.

Column

Also known as a sheath, this is a slim-cut dress (although not particularly fitted) often made in a plain fabric such as crepe that drops straight to the floor.

Great for: You incredible willowy glamazons who run (or look like they run) 10km a day, as this dress follows the natural curves of a bride's body.

Avoid if: You are like me and conscious of your curves. These dresses are often made in a plain fabric so combine that with the slim fit of the dress, and there is nowhere to hide!

A basque skirt combined with a square neckline is perfect for creating a soft, romantic look.

This column dress has a bardot neckline that sits just off the shoulders to show the top of the arms. It's great for showing off necklaces, but avoid these if you feel you have broader arms as it can cut you off at the widest part.

Drop Waist

The bodice of the drop-waist dress style is similar to that of a basque, but it drops a little further past the natural waistline and down toward the hips.

Great for: Those of you who are blessed with small hips.

Avoid if: You are petite as it can make you look even shorter.

Empire

This one always reminds me of *Pride and Prejudice* but in a good way! This shape of dress has a much higher waistline that starts under the boobs, right on the bit where the underwire of your bra is. The skirt is long and flowing…perfect for running into the arms of Mr. Darcy!

Great for: Anyone who feels their body shape is on the rounder side and needs some waist definition, but wants to draw attention away from their legs. This is also perfect if you're not blessed with large bosoms; this shape is fab for giving you some oomph.

Avoid if: I find this shape flattering for pretty much everyone, but I do sometimes find that if a bride's boobs are on the larger side they can sometimes look like a medieval beer wench (think Nancy from *Oliver Twist*).

This drop-waist dress has a halterneck – a dress with no sleeves that usually fastens at the back of the neck, with deep cut armholes showing off the shoulders and top of the arms. A halterneck is great if you have broad shoulders as it accentuates the collarbone.

This off-the-shoulder neckline matches the elegance of an empire-cut dress.

Fishtail

I think the best way to describe this shape is to imagine a child's drawing of a fish. You know the one, with the round body and a sort of triangular tail? That's pretty much exactly how this shape of dress looks. A fitted dress that flares out at the knee. Like a cartoon fish!

Great for: Hourglass brides as it accentuates curves in the best possible way. Also for petite brides as the shape can elongate the figure and create the illusion of a longer body. Slim brides too as the shape can give you gives if you haven't really got them!

Avoid if: You have a rounder, apple-shaped figure as this dress shape can draw attention to the curves that you may not want to emphasise.

This fishtail dress has a plunge neckline – a deep V that starts from the shoulders and comes to meet anywhere from the cleavage to the belly button!

A great neckline if you're petite, as a plunge can make you look taller and longer.

These are little off-the-shoulder straps which give the effect of a bardot neckline. I add them to my brides dresses all the time as it's such a simple tweak to a dress that elevates it to perfection. They're also great to add if, like me, you hate the tops of your arms.

Mermaid, aka Fit and Flare

This is the more paired-down sister of a fishtail. The best way to describe this shape is to get you to imagine the shape of a mermaid's tail. The Mermaid or Fit and Flare shape dress is fitted from the bodice down towards the mid-thigh area into a more subtly flared skirt. The flare is just above the knee on mermaid dresses, whereas it's just below the knee on fishtails.

Great for: Another shape that works beautifully on pear-shaped and hourglass figures as it makes your curves look *fiiiiiiiinnnnne*!

Avoid if: You consider yourself more apple-shaped as it can draw attention to your belly.

Tea Length

Tea Length: Named after the tea parties they were traditionally designed to be worn for, this style dress is basically a shorter version of all her sisters.

Great for: This style looks fab on every bride, but is particularly great for petite brides.

This mermaid dress has a Bateau or boat neckline, one that is cut from shoulder to shoulder, straight across the collarbone.

This tea-length dress has an illusion neckline, with its flesh-coloured piece of tulle (mesh) that is added to the dress to give the appearance of less coverage than there actually is. You will tend to find an illusion section added to the bodice of a dress, for example, to make a plunge look less "plungey". This is a great option if you want a little more coverage around your chest or decolletage area without completely hiding it.

Short Wedding Dress

I don't think I need to explain what a short dress is, do I!?

These are great for a civil ceremony or a destination wedding. You can even change into a short wedding dress for your evening reception, but bear in mind that by the time you do this, the majority of your guests will probably be pissed and won't even notice. So I would really consider if it's worth the extra expense.

This modern little piece combines a bustier top with a short skirt.

Chapter Takeaways

Be open-minded. If you absolutely *hate* the look of a dress on the hanger then it's unlikely you're going to love it when you try it on. However, if you're just feeling unsure about it, then I definitely recommend that you try her. Chances are, you'll be pleasantly surprised!

Boutiques aren't expecting you to have put together a "Monica" from *Friends* type of portfolio that shows your wedding day and wedding dress vision, but it is really useful to have a few ideas about what style of dresses you like the look of and ones that you don't.

This is also why it's so important to have your venue booked before you go dress shopping. The perfect wedding dress for a classic wedding in the British countryside will be very different from the perfect dress for a beach wedding in the baking hot Jamaican sun.

Head to the glossary at the back of this book if you need a quick reference guide to all the dress shapes and necklines.

Chapter 4
Let's Get Naked!

90% of being married is shouting "What?" from other rooms.

Putting a wedding dress on your body is the most surreal feeling ever! We know it's coming as soon as we get that ring on our finger, but nothing prepares you for how weird it feels (in a good way, obviously!).

Once you've gotten over the weirdness, I promise you'll relax into things and the fun will begin. In this chapter, I'll talk you through the next stage of the appointment process so that you can chill out and enjoy the experience in the way that we (bridal boutiques) want you to.

Getting Naked

We're human. No matter our shape – curvy and petite, willowy and tall (I hate you) – we all have our body hang-ups and insecurities. The pressure we put on ourselves to look a specific way when we get married is *insane*. Your fiancé loves you for *you*, not because of how they think you could potentially look if your body shape changed, you got a six-pack and magically lost all your body hair.

Likewise, believe me when I tell you bridal stylists have seen it all before. We honestly could not give two shits about how you look, whether you have had a pedicure or a bikini wax etc, etc. I have had countless sets of boobs in my face over the last decade and have lost count of the number of times I have been face to fanny, and I promise you I really *don't* care! The only thing we all want is for you to relax and enjoy yourself.

These anxieties have no place taking up prime real estate in your head, so please don't allow them to ruin this wonderful experience for you.

What to Wear

Again, something else that you really do not need to stress your pretty little head about, but here are a few tips…

Clothes. I would advise wearing minimal layers or loose clothes that are easy to get on and off. You don't want to waste the first

30 minutes of your appointment trying to get out of your leather jeggings a la Ross in *Friends!*

Makeup. We don't expect you to attend your dress appointment completely bare-faced (I would not grace the threshold of Tesco's without at least concealer and mascara on my face...and maybe bronzer...and a touch of blusher). However, please remember that boutiques have had to invest a huge amount of money into these gowns. They need to look fresh and new for as long as we can keep them that way to ensure that every bride is able to try a dress that is as immaculate as it was when it first landed in the boutique. Self-tan stains on the lining, foundation marks around the neckline, lipstick on the cuff...none of these scream "luxury shopping experience," do they?

So when it comes to makeup, we just ask that you be mindful with the amount you apply. Ultimately, there's only one place that bright red Mac lipstick is going, and that's smeared right across the front of that white dress.

Underwear. Pale (ideally white or flesh-coloured) knickers are the best thing to wear, but if you really haven't got any then just wear the lightest colour you can find in your knicker drawer. Don't give us the sob story "I can't tell what the dress looks like because I'm distracted by my underwear" if you rock up to your appointment in black and fuschia leopard-print pants.

If you're blessed with a decent rack, then a well-fitted, pale-coloured strapless bra is great, but please don't go out and buy one especially.

Deodorant. I'm hoping this is fairly obvious, but if not, please bear in mind that your bridal consultant will pretty much have their face in your armpit for a huge portion of your appointment. Although, historically, brides carried a bouquet of flowers to disguise the horrific smell of their body odour, I really don't think we need to keep this tradition alive.

Jewellery. If you're planning on keeping your bridal jewellery to a minimum on your wedding day, then it may be a good idea to just wear something simple (if any at all), to your appointment. And please, for the love of all things bridal, *take off that bloody smartwatch!*

Shoes. I'd be surprised if the boutique you are booked to visit doesn't have a suitable pair of shoes for you to wear when you are trying on dresses. However, I can't speak for everyone, which is why it may be a good idea to check with the store beforehand if you will be expected to bring your own shoes with you.

Please don't rely on standing barefoot on a box or small podium to give you the same impression of wearing heels as it really isn't the same. Heels, no matter the height, give you a different sort of posture – a chin-up, shoulders-back, tits-out posture that standing on a box simply can't do.

Trying on Your First Dress

So, first things first: I just want to remind you that wedding dress shop samples *rarely* fit any bride perfectly. Dresses are pretty much always too big or too small. Some fit great around the boobs, but (like me) you can't get it up and over your generous backside. Or it's looking lovely around your hips and bum, but your melons are cascading over the neckline like a medieval wench. Whatever the fit, please remember that this is not how your dress will look on your wedding day and an experienced stylist should be able to expertly clip or pin you into the dress so that you'll be able to get a good idea of how it is designed to look and feel.

A historic way of helping shop samples look better on a bride is to shove a sponge down the back of a dress to fill any gaps. If a stylist tries to do this to you, then I advise ripping the sponge from her hand and throwing it across the fitting room whilst yelling a firm but assertive "NO" at them. If you feel you need to wag your finger at this point, then please do so.

All this technique does is make you look like the Hunchback of Notre Dame.

It won't be perfect, but this is when you need to follow your gut instinct: If you're getting butterflies, feeling giddy and can start to visualise yourself walking down the aisle in a dress (more on this later!) then you're onto a winner. But if you can't see past the sample fit, the pinned straps or the clips around your waist, then chances are it's not your dress.

I often compare this to house buying…random I know, but bear with me on this. If you're viewing a house and can't see past the brown bathroom suite, the overgrown gardens or the shiny purple wallpaper, then you know it's not your dream home. However, if you walk into a shack that pretty much resembles a crack den and can, at once, visualise where the reclaimed fireplace will go or how pretty the floorboards will be after you've peeled back the sticky carpet, then you know this property has something special. It feels *right*.

That said, you need to be honest with your bridal stylist. I promise that our intention isn't to interrogate you, and we really don't want you to feel awkward. But we are here to help you and we honestly do care about you and your opinions. It's our job to help you find a wedding dress that is unparalleled beyond compare and we won't quit until we have completed our mission!

So, if you are standing there in a dress that you dislike, then don't just tell them that; try and explain *why*. You don't necessarily need to go into a huge amount of detail with your feedback, but by giving us some high-level likes and dislikes, you will enable us to find an alternative dress that may just end up being absolutely perfect.

It's also super important that you don't shop for the dress size that you want or hope to wear on your wedding day. You are putting unnecessary pressure on yourself and should love how you look in your dress at that exact moment (I didn't lose a pound for either of my weddings and was happily spooning Pizza Express garlic butter into my mouth the night before I married my first husband. I could not have cared less about my weight).

If you want to lose a few inches and you manage to do so, then that's just bloody marvellous (seriously...how did you do it?). But there's no point trying on fishtail dresses that look less than perfect right now in the hope that the dress shape will be perfect on your wedding day, because you have manifested a seven-stone weight loss. It's not realistic and it is not fair on your mental health. What *is* realistic is how you look and feel right now.

"The stylists encouraged me to try a dress that I thought was the opposite of what I wanted, but it ended up being The One! I loved how I looked in this dress at that exact moment, so much so that even if I didn't lose any more weight I knew I would still feel fabulous, which also took a huge amount of pressure off me.

I am getting married next Friday and can't wait to see it all together!

– Real bride, Suzii

Dress Additions

It's certainly commonplace now to make tweaks or add little elements to a dress to elevate it to the status of "perfection." My team is always adding straps or sleeves, closing in necklines, lowering backs, extending the length of trains and so on. It's generally pretty easy to do and a skilled seamstress shouldn't have a problem doing this for you, but be prepared for additional charges to your alterations bill. Alternatively, your dress designer may have a service that includes doing these additions to the dress during the production process, but I've found that this is more the exception than the rule. Either way, your stylist will be able to talk you through the best (and most cost-effective) way of doing this.

An important thing to note here is that making tweaks and additions to a dress in order to make it perfect for you is great. However, if you are finding yourself saying "If we change the neckline, remove all the lace, add sleeves, lower the back...then it will be perfect," then it's probably not the dress for you. An experienced stylist should be able to listen to what you are saying and trot off to find you a dress that is more in line with what you're looking for. The odd tweak or addition to taking a dress from a 9.99 to a 10 out of 10 is absolutely fine. But if you need to completely change it, then I would suggest it's not your dream dress and you need to keep looking.

Obviously please disregard this bit of the book if you're having a dress designed especially for you and to your specifications, as that is the whole point of having a bespoke gown!

Alllll the Opinions

As I mentioned previously, too many cooks make wedding dress shopping a bloody nightmare, so please consider your guest list wisely.

I've met traditional mothers who consider a split in a skirt or a slightly plunged neckline practically pornographic. I've met "modern" mums (think Amy Poehler in *Mean Girls*: "I'm not a regular mom, I'm a cool mom!") who have suggested that *they* try on the dresses to help the bride make a decision. I've met spiteful elder sisters who are so jealous that the baby of the family is getting married before her and cannot bear to say anything helpful, let alone complimentary (one even pulled a book from her bag and sat and read throughout the appointment). I've met the bridesmaid who recently got married herself and who just cannot *wait* to impart *allllll* of her knowledge and opinions to any other bride she meets…

The list goes on and on and on and on.

All I have to do is remind you that this is *your* appointment. *Your* experience. *Your* wedding dress. If you can't stand your mother-in-law, then don't invite her to come dress shopping with you. If you love your sister, but wouldn't ask her opinion on pizza toppings let alone fashion advice, don't invite her. If you have 324 bridesmaids, but you really only care about the opinion of your best friend or maid of honour, then don't invite the others!

I promise you that too many guests mean too many opinions. There has never been a situation in my boutique where we have found that having 13 different opinions was actually really helpful and not confusing at all! Guests often think they are being supportive by picking dresses they think are great for the bride. But whether they realise it or not, the dresses they choose are usually ones *they* like, as opposed to what they think will look good on you, The Bride.

Likewise, if the gang exclaims, "Urgh! No way!" before the bride has even opened her mouth and given her own opinion, then it's usually because all they are focusing on is their own personal feelings about the dress, and not on how the dress looks on the bride.

You have obviously brought these guests with you on your dress-shopping journey because you love them and you value their opinions. But please remember that it's your dress and your decision. Finding your dream dress should only be about how *you* feel. Your opinion is the only one that matters

This is your opportunity to be selfish. Just tell everyone that you want your dress to be a surprise for them, or simply blame the store you intend to visit and tell the girls that you are only allowed to take two guests with you to your appointment. Otherwise, you would of course invite them too! Don't worry Bridey, we've got your back, and we are more than happy to go along with any necessary white lies, if it means that you will have the exciting and fun shopping experience that you deserve.

And on statements like, "Try this one on for a laugh!" or "OMG! Bridey just *has* to try this dress on! It's not at all what she wants and she won't like it, but it'll be really funny!" I beg you, on behalf of all bridal boutiques, please don't let your entourage do this. It's really fucking annoying.

I know how overwhelming all this dress trying becomes, so scribble down these questions to remind you or one of your gang to ask your stylist:

- Please can I try sitting down in my dress?

- Does the dress have a bustle for the evening and if not, will a seamstress add one for me?

- How well would this dress travel? (If applicable).

- What shoes and accessories would you suggest?

I would also advise a bride against heavily embellished or jewelled shoes if they are wearing a tulle skirt, or if their dress has tulle underskirts, as the fabric will catch on them.

Chapter Takeaways

Do not waste time worrying about how you look naked. We honestly don't care if you've plucked every single pubic hair from your bikini line or if you haven't changed your chipped toenail varnish in seven months. Just take your damn clothes off and get into the dress!

The dresses that you try arc unlikely to fit you perfectly. An experienced stylist should be able to clip and pin them so that you'll get a better idea of how the dress will look and feel when it is in a more appropriate size and has been altered sufficiently.

If you can't see past the less-than-ideal fit of a sample dress, then chances are it's not your dress. Move on to the next.

Making little additions or tweaks to your dress to take it from a 9.9 to a 20 out of 10 is completely normal and fairly simple to do. However, if you're finding yourself wanting to make lots of changes then it's not your dress. You shouldn't have to change a dress to make yourself like it.

It's YOUR dress. It's YOUR decision.

So you've got the dress on, you're loving it, you feel blimmin' gorgeous, it's everything you were hoping for and more! But the only problem is that no one is crying! That must mean that this exquisite gown can't be The One then, no?

Crikey, we really do convince ourselves of a load of bull, don't we!? The "Crying Myth" is just one of many misconceptions that bridal stylists battle on a daily basis, so in the next chapter I am going to take you through each myth and smash the shit out of them so that you can choose your dress based on nothing other than how *you feel* in it.

Chapter 5
"But Why Aren't You Crying?!"

Marriage is like a walk in the park...Jurassic Park.

This is it. This is the moment you've been waiting for.

You're standing there in front of the mirror and can't quite believe what is happening.

You didn't know what you were looking for in a wedding dress and yet here it is in all its glory! You feel incredible, you feel beautiful, you feel confident and you can visualise yourself walking down the aisle toward your fiancé. Everything has fallen into place. You feel a sense of calm certainty that this is *the* dress...the one that truly reflects you as a person...your authentic self.

This is *your* moment.

And then...

"Oh, Bridey! You can't say yes to the dress at your first shop! Even if you know it's The One, because my auntie's neighbour has a friend who knows her cleaner, and she said that the cashier in Aldi told her that she visited 372 shops before ordering her dress. Even if it did end up being the very first one she tried!"

And that's it. A member of your entourage has just shat all over your perfect moment.

You found your dream dress and were about to say *"Yes."* But then, one of your friends or relatives decided to be *helpful.* At this precise moment, they shared some bollocks they heard on the grapevine – or saw on *Say Yes To The Dress* – and completely sucked all the magic and excitement out of your experience.

So, this chapter is where I tell you to ignore everything anyone says. I'm going to dispel all of the stupid myths and so-called "rules" that are thrown at brides before they even book their first bridal shop appointment. That way, when any of your guests try to helpfully impart their words of wisdom upon you (because that's what *she* did when *she* went dress shopping), you can turn around and confidently tell them to "bog off" because you know what they're saying is utter bullshit.

Myth 1: "If you aren't moved to tears, then it's not your dress."

Really? *Really?!* Look, I've been married twice, and not once have I cried over my wedding dresses. I'm not an overly emotional person, but I'm not made of stone either (although my lovely ex-husband may argue this point). I, of course, felt *something*. However, I can absolutely confirm that I don't tend to cry at clothing – unless I'm in a Zara fitting room and have gotten myself stuck in yet another dress that is too small for me. So the fact that I wasn't crying when I was in a wedding dress certainly didn't put me off ordering it. My mother didn't cry, my friends didn't cry (bitches) and yet I still wasn't deterred because I *knew* it was The One.

How did I know? Because I felt amazing! Despite the sample being too small for me, the zip wouldn't go up and my arse was hanging out the back, I could still visualise myself getting married in it.

Not all brides are criers. It's OK if you're not one of them.

Myth 2: "I can't order this dress…it's my first shop!"

Okay, so you're on a yacht. The sun is setting. Your gorgeous boyfriend is down on one knee and a dolphin leaps out of the waves with a stunning solitaire diamond ring on its tongue. He smoothly takes it from the creature, and finally, *finally*, your boyfriend asks that question you've been waiting seven years for.

Now, do you answer with, "Potentially, I am going to say yes; However, I really do feel that I need to test out a few other partners before I commit to you. You know, just to make sure." Or do you say, "Can I come back to you with my answer after I've tried out a few others? Because you never know. I've heard that Barry in Newcastle or Leanne in Dublin is fit and could be The One."

No. You don't. Because you didn't think for one second that there was any answer other than "Yes!" You didn't question it. You didn't think, "What if there is something better out there?" You can't explain what it is about them, they're just perfect for you. So you say, "I do."

Now I'm not comparing your fiancé to a wedding dress. But I *am* trying to help you appreciate just how ridiculous this sounds to bridal boutiques: When you find the dress of your absolute dreams but are too scared to order it. Why? Because you've only visited one shop and are worried there will be a better dress out there.

Industry data tells us that over 70% of brides find their dress at the first shop they visit.

Let me tell you that if you keep shopping, you will just keep finding variations of the dress that you loved at your first shop. I've had many brides over the years return to my boutique after shopping around, ready to order the dress they initially loved at their first appointment, only to find that the gown they wanted has been discontinued or that their chosen designer won't be able to make the dress in time for their wedding date due to strict production lead times. These brides missed out on the dress of their dreams simply because they became so consumed with searching for something that *could* be better. FOMO is a cruel mistress.

I completely understand that unsettling feeling you think you may have when you commit to your dress…like it's the end of a chapter. But just remind yourself of that incredible feeling you had when you found yourself in the perfect dress.

There will *always* be more wedding dresses. There will *always* be more men, but you have to stop somewhere!

> *"I didn't ever believe people when they tell you that when you try on The One you instantly know, but I'm now a huge believer of this. I found The One in the first and only ever bridal shop I went into! I now always tell people it doesn't matter if it's the first shop you go into, if it's The One, then get the dress!*
>
> *Finding my wedding dress is my favourite memory of planning my wedding and I'll forever be thankful to Tilly's for making it so fantastic!"*
>
> *– Real bride, Lucy*

Myth 3: "I didn't plan on ordering my dress today," or "I didn't expect to find my dress today."

Okay, let's say you need a gorgeous outfit for an event. You trot off to your nearest shopping centre, go to the first shop on your list and you see it right there, gazing down at you from the mannequin – the perfect outfit. Exactly what you were looking for. Plus, they have one left in your size. Bonus!

Do you then think, "Well this is perfect! However, I didn't think I'd be lucky enough to find an outfit today, even though I came shopping with the intention of finding one. So I'm going to go home and then look again in a few weeks."

No, you don't.

You pick it up, take it to the cashier and then spend the rest of your day having a stress-free mooch around the beauty hall, perusing cute little bookshops or simply getting pissed on pornstar martinis in the nearest bar.

To have a bride stand in front of us in the most incredible gown, see her cry with happiness because she has never felt as beautiful as she does right there at that moment, and then to hear the words, "I need to go away and think about things as I didn't plan on finding my dress today," – it blows our little minds! If you didn't *plan* on finding your wedding dress after you've gone out of your way to gather your nearest and dearest, coordinate a date and book an appointment at a bridal boutique, then why the hell are you shopping?

Likewise, you may not expect to find your dream dress in the first, second or tenth shop you visit, but I promise you, my loves, you *will* find a dress. Wedding dresses feel like nothing you have ever worn before and you will become besotted.

Do us all a favour, Brideys. If you have absolutely no intention of ordering your wedding dress yet, please don't start shopping.

Myth 4: "I'm scared that if I order too early, I'll regret my decision or change my mind."

The only questions you need to ask yourself are:

"Do I feel beautiful?"

"Can I imagine myself getting married in this?"

"Do I feel like me, but better?"

If the answer is "Yes," then you've found your dress! Yay! Now you can go ahead and delete the Pinterest board, chuck away the bridal magazines (do they even exist anymore?) and unfollow those Instagram accounts you've been obsessing over. You have found The One.

If you have chosen a dress based solely on how *you* feel as opposed to what your friends say, whether your mum likes it, whether it's similar to Sophie Habboo or Kim Kardashian's dress, then I promise you won't regret it. Use your gut, my loves. Your intuition won't lead you astray.

I'm not going to promise you that you won't have a wobble after you've ordered your dress. It's completely normal and happens all the time, particularly when there is so much choice out there. If you're really panicking, then contact the team at your chosen bridal boutique and see if you can pop back in to try your gown on again, to remind yourself just how besotted you are with her.

I can, hand on heart, assure you that if you follow my guidance you will love your dress just as much on your wedding day as you do the day that you order it. If not more!

"When I saw the dress on the mannequin, I had such an exciting feeling that no other dress I saw made me feel.

When I stepped in, pulled it up and the stylist pinned me in, I absolutely felt like I was floating. The joy I felt is still incomparable. You say to trust your gut and I totally agree. Something in your bones just knows it's yours."

– Real bride, Tara

Myth 5: "If you don't have a "proper" dress for your wedding, then it's not a wedding dress."

Oh, don't be so bloody ridiculous.

Myth 6: "My best friend told me that I have to take photos of every dress I try on so that I can go back and remember them all, even the ones I don't like."

Does this friend also advise that you keep photos of every person you have dated and sit and analyse every single one so that you can remember each of them? Even the absolute dickheads? No, I didn't think so. And if any of your friends do suggest this, my advice is to rethink your friendship group.

A badly lit photo taken at a gross angle on a camera phone (usually taken by your poor mum whilst you yell at her for not standing up) is really not how you should be remembering your beautiful gown. A photo won't truly capture how you *feel* and it really is that feeling – those butterflies in the pit of your belly – that you should be relying on to remind you of your magnificent dress.

It's not uncommon for boutiques to ban photography during appointments and that can be for a number of reasons. Like me, they don't want you to have a dodgy photo as the lasting memory of when you found The One. The lighting will be unflattering, you are unlikely to be wearing your hair and make-up in exactly the same way as you will on your wedding day, the sample won't fit you properly…the list of cons is endless!

As I didn't work in the bridal industry when I married my first husband, I was completely oblivious to all of these factors and merrily snapped away. I had ordered my dress two years before my wedding date, so I then spent the following 24 months staring at those pictures. By the time the day came around for me to finally go back to the boutique to try *my* dress, that feeling of elation had significantly diminished.

Don't get me wrong, I was still over the moon and completely besotted with my dress, but that giddy excitement I had when I found my gown definitely wasn't as prevalent.

In addition to this, I had also spent two years showing these photos to pretty much anyone who made eye contact with me. Everyone responded with the "Ooohs" and "Ahhhs" that were expected of them – except for one who said, "Oh! I didn't expect you to wear something like that." It was not the most offensive of retorts, but it was enough to strike fear into my very soul. Subsequently, I spent the following months questioning my dress choice.

When the wedding day came around and I burst out of the bedroom to present my incredible self to my bridesmaids, none of them even batted an eyelid – another scenario that left a bitter taste in my mouth. They would never have admitted it, but having spent the last two years being repeatedly shown the same picture, they were so *over* my dress.

Now, my second wedding was a different story. I didn't show a *soul*. I didn't even take a photo of myself in it to be able to show anyone. Yes, this was because I now knew the risks that I wasn't aware of the first time around. But also (and most importantly) I simply couldn't care less what other people thought. I adored my outfit and that's all that mattered.

Myth 7: "You should always sleep on it before you say 'Yes.'"

In my opinion (and this is my book so I can keep giving you my opinions!), if you feel you should step away from your dress, if you feel that your "Yes" isn't instant and unforced, or if you feel that you need to have a sleepless night weighing up the pros and cons of said dress, then it probably isn't your dress.

Did you need to sleep on it when your fiancé asked you to marry them?!

Chapter Takeaways

Just because you, your mum, your bridesmaids or the lady who works in Sainsbury's didn't cry when you found The One, doesn't mean it's not The One.

Just because you find The One at the first bridal shop you visit, it does not mean that you can't order it.

You don't have to visit 3,775 bridal shops before you can actually commit to a dress.

If you have no intention of ordering your wedding dress yet, then don't start shopping.

You *will* fall in love with a wedding dress. So be prepared.

When you find your dress, stop looking. It is that simple.

Wobbles and "buyer's remorse" are completely normal, but if you follow your instinct and order a dress that makes you feel absolutely incredible, then I *promise* you won't regret it.

There is no such thing as a "proper" wedding dress. It's your day… wear whatever the hell you want.

So now that you feel confident enough to stick two fingers up to any "helpful" advice or suggestions that any friends and family feel they need to impart to you when you are about to say "Yes!" to your dress, we can move on to what happens next in your wedding dress journey…

Chapter 6
To Veil or Not to Veil?

Behind every great man is a woman rolling her eyes.

You've done it! I knew you could! How amazing are you feeling right now?

You've managed to find your dream wedding dress in a glorious bridal boutique, supported by incredible bridal stylists and in the presence of your nearest and dearest. Bliss!

So, what happens now?

This is by no means the end of your wedding dress journey. If anything, it is just the beginning. I'm here to talk you through those next steps so that by the end of this chapter you will be able to relax knowing that the most important element – your dream dress – has been sorted. Then, if you are content with the dress making her statement alone without any of the bells and whistles – veils, hair accessories, jewellery – you can skip a page or two to the section about veils. However, if you are still deciding on those finishing touches ("Can I wear a hairpiece *and* a veil *and* statement jewellery without it looking over the top?") then read on and I'll guide you through the minefield of bridal accessories.

Shoes and veils and jewellery! Oh my!

Shoes

There are two trains of thought when it comes to bridal shoes and I can appreciate both sides. Some say that there is absolutely no point in spending loads of money on your bridal shoes because no one sees them…which is true to an extent.

I spent a fortune on my wedding shoes (Jimmy Choo for both weddings…obvs). I don't regret it one bit because *I* knew I had amazing artwork on my Tilly Trotters (feet) and that is all I needed. I couldn't care less who saw them and who didn't because *I* loved them.

Ultimately, the thing to remember is that, realistically, your guests are only going to see the front of your shoe, and that is only going to be when you walk. This makes me ask: Do you really want your guests to be staring at your feet all day just so they can appreciate your bridal shoes?

What I'm trying to say is that you can either spend a fortune on your wedding shoes or you can get an equally fabulous pair from the High Street (Dune offers some amazing bridal shoe collections). It doesn't matter either way, as long as the height is manageable and the style is comfortable.

Oh, and a side note: If you have a tulle skirt or lots of tulle (net) underskirts, please don't invest in a fancy pair of jewelled or embellished shoes as they will just catch on the fabric. At the very least, they'll do your head in; at worst, they'll rip the skirt of your dress. Not okay.

Hair Accessories

The options for hair accessories are endless. There are so many to choose from and, if I'm honest, you really don't need to spend a fortune to get something beautiful.

A lot of bridal boutiques have a huge amount of variety and options, but in my opinion…a hair slide is a hair slide. Unless you want something really specific and bespoke, don't waste your life analysing 567 different variations of the same hairband and just go with the prettiest option. Chances are you will find something perfect and *very* reasonably priced on websites like Etsy.

Jewellery

Basically, unless you have an item of jewellery that holds a huge amount of sentimental value, I really wouldn't bother spending the equivalent of a year's mortgage on a pair of diamond earrings. Unless, of course, you want to.

I truly feel that nothing is more elegant than a naked decolletage and a pair of chic earrings to complete a bride's ensemble.

(Oh, and bear in mind that bracelets have a tendency to catch on dresses and snag the fabric, so I always encourage brides to avoid wearing one if possible.)

To Veil or Not to Veil...

...That is the question! I didn't wear a veil for either of my weddings and I really regret it. In my opinion, your wedding is really your only opportunity to wear such a dramatic accessory. (Although there are no rules; if you want to buy a veil and wear it on the school run, then go for it. You do you, my love.) So why not make the most of being a bride and accessorise with aplomb?

Historians tell us that wedding veils were traditionally worn by brides during the Ancient Greek and Roman times as it was believed they gave protection from the evil spirits who wanted to stand in her way of happiness. As time moved on, veils became less about protection and more of a symbol of a bride's virtue and chastity.

Nowadays, veils are more often worn as a styling addition rather than for any symbolic reason, and the designs have really evolved. Be gone, gross, old-fashioned styles of veils that are shapeless and made from horrible crunchy tulle! These days, there are endless options and you can absolutely find one that beautifully complements your wedding gown.

If you're looking to make a dramatic entrance that instigates gasps of wonderment from your guests, then try a cathedral-length veil. This is the most formal style of veil and the length generally extends past the train of a wedding dress – ensuring optimum drama! They could be embroidered, have a touch of sparkle or beadwork and be trimmed with ribbon or lace. Likewise, cathedral-length veils look equally stunning when they have no additions except for a simple raw (cut) edge.

One of my brides had a simple, elegant cathedral-length veil with a raw edge, but then added her personality by embroidering along the base of the veil (in fuschia pink) the lyrics to her and her fiancé's favourite song. The options really are endless!

If you're finding cathedral length a little too much but you're still looking to make a statement, then you may want to consider a chapel-length veil. These are still long (usually around 90 inches from comb to end), but don't extend as far past the train of the dress compared to cathedral length.

A two-tier, cathedral-length veil. Don't you love the drama?

For ultimate drama, you should try a two-tier veil, which is basically a veil of any length with a blusher covering your face. A blusher is designed to be lifted away from the bride's face to reveal her as her father gives her away to her groom, or alternatively at the end of the wedding ceremony when the bride and groom kiss.

I *love* the theatrical element that a blusher gives to a bride's overall look. However, I do have to confess that the thought of relying on a man to lift a blusher without messing my hair up or smearing lip gloss across my face fills me with utter dread! Just something to bear in mind, loves!

A two-tier, elbow-length veil

If you are looking for a more stylised look, then shorter veils could be the way to go. Shoulder length and elbow length are pretty self-explanatory, but I have always considered birdcage veils to be incredibly cool. These are 1940s-inspired veils and supposedly came about in the postwar era due to fabric shortages. They are typically made from Russian net or tulle and usually reach down no further than your cheeks or chin.

A shoulder-length veil

A birdcage veil

My advice is to try on all styles of veils to see which one you prefer and then go from there. My boutique offers our brides the opportunity to attend a Styling Appointment, whereby the girls can visit the boutique to try *their* dress once it has arrived and test out all other styling options – jewellery, shoes, hairpieces and so on. It is also the ideal opportunity to test the waters with veils and not only select the best style to complement your gown but to also decide if you actually want to wear one at all.

Even though it's not a huge amount of money to spend in the grand scheme of weddings (just note that the more you add and the more elaborate the veil, generally the more expensive), it is still a chunk of money that could be used on booze rather than spent on an accessory that you aren't overly fussed about wearing.

If you try a veil on and it just feels really weird, awkward and not you, then don't wear one and save your money! As I've said on numerous occasions, there are no rules when it comes to your bridal style. Don't let any well-meaning bridesmaid, friend or mother bully you into or out of anything you do or do not want to do.

So now that your accessories are sorted, we just need to do something about the length of your dress, because it's clearly been made for a 20ft supermodel. Actually, the shoulders could do with lifting slightly…and the waist taken in a bit. Let's talk alterations….

Chapter 7
"I'm Sorry, What? You're Cutting My Dress?"

When you see a couple walking down the street, the one who's a few steps ahead is the one who's mad.

So, let us assume that you've been a good little bridey and you have ordered your stunning wedding dress months in advance. Consequently, we now have plenty of time for stress-free alterations.

A question we are frequently asked is, "Why do we need alterations? Won't my dress be ready for me to wear as soon as it arrives?"

The simple answer is "No!" And let me explain why.

Made to Measure vs. Made to Order

There are generally two prominent methods of production when it comes to making wedding dresses – Made to Order (MTO) or Made to Measure (MTM).

The most common service is MTO, a process where a wedding dress is made to a *standard* size according to a designer's size chart. Generally, three measurements will be taken – bust, waist and hip – then the most appropriate size according to the relevant designer's size chart will be selected for you.

First and foremost, a standard size in bridal is very different from a standard size on the High Street. Bridal can often come up a lot smaller, and so if you are a 12 in H&M (that's probably a bad example as H&M sizing is so fucked up, it's ridiculous), don't be surprised if you match up to a different number on a particular wedding dress designer's size chart.

Secondly, we are often split size (i.e. split between two or three sizes). Your hip measurement may be a certain size while your bust measurement is another. If you do find yourself in a situation where you are perhaps falling between a size 12 and 14, then the boutique would usually advise that it is better (and safer) to order your dress in a size 14 and then tailor it to fit. It is *much* easier to alter a wedding dress and take it in to make it smaller, rather than letting it out.

For example, my wedding dress came out as a size 16 even though I am a 12 to 14 in my "normal" clothes. This is not to say that I am always a size 16 in bridal; it simply means that my biggest *measurement* was a size 16.

At the end of the day, I couldn't care less what size my clothes are, bridal or otherwise. All I wanted for my wedding was to look the absolute best I possibly could – a goal your bridal seamstress should help you reach. Plus, it's not like the size label is going to be dangling out the back of your dress when you walk down the aisle, nor are your guests likely to storm out when they see you are wearing a size 12 dress when they always thought you were a size 8!

Some bridal designers offer an MTM option: A custom wedding gown that is made to your exact body measurements. However, this is based on an existing design that is then made to fit your body shape and not a *bespoke* design made to your specifications. A stylist will take a lot of measurements (approximately 20), send them off to the designer and you will return to the boutique a period of time later for your muslin or toile fitting. A muslin or toile is a dress pattern that is essentially a basic cotton prototype of your final dress. At this fitting, your designer or bridal stylist will discuss the *fit* of the dress to make sure you are happy and discuss any design changes before they go ahead and make the final dress.

MTM is often a more expensive service as the work involved is so intrinsic and time-consuming. It is also worth bearing in mind that a designer has absolutely no control over your weight and body measurements. So if your weight fluctuates (or if, like me, you just got fatter as the engagement progressed), please don't expect to get away without having to pay for additional alterations once your dress is completed and delivered to the boutique.

I used to stock a designer in my boutique that offered both MTM and MTO options. One of my brides opted to pay an additional, significant amount for her dress to be MTM. She then went through so many weight fluctuations over the months leading up to her wedding that she had to fork out almost double that amount again for an independent seamstress to alter her dress.

Please just keep all of this in mind if you're considering an MTM service.

 Obviously, please disregard this bit of the book if you're having a dress designed especially for you and to your specifications, as that is the whole point of having a bespoke gown!

How to Find a Bridal Seamstress

Please – and I cannot emphasise this enough – only use a *recommended* bridal seamstress. Plucking a number out of the Yellow Pages (which is an old-fashioned phone book to all you Gen Z's out there) with no knowledge of their experience or reputation is simply a wedding dress disaster waiting to happen.

I had a bride who insisted on having a family friend alter her wedding dress rather than our recommendation and as it turns out, the friend was a menswear tailor and not specifically a bridal seamstress. The tailor didn't understand the cut, the construction nor the design of different wedding dresses and ultimately butchered my bride's dress. She ended up having to get married in our shop sample rather than her own gown.

I'm not aware of any bridal shop that isn't connected to an experienced bridal seamstress in some way or other. Some boutiques employ an "in-house" seamstress, which means that they work solely for one boutique. Others have a little black book of wonder women and men from which you can choose who will work their magic on your precious cargo.

If a boutique has no one to recommend, then I would advise that you hit up your newly married friends or even another bridal shop and see if they have a seamstress. Just remember to go by *recommendation*.

How Much Do Alterations Cost?

Ah, the million-dollar question! Well, how long is a piece of string? The cost of alterations can vary quite significantly, depending on the complexity of the work.

Alterations on heavily embellished or lace dresses will generally cost more. Location is also a big factor to consider; you will almost certainly be paying more for your alterations within the London area. Different seamstresses charge different amounts for their services and I really don't want to do any of them out of some money by undervaluing them in this book! I recommend budgeting around £500 to be on the safe side, but your seamstress will provide you with a bespoke quotation at your first fitting.

However, let me give you some insight as a rough guide:

Standard alterations (such as altering the hem, adjusting the straps, adding a bustle, taking in the bust and altering the waist) should be at the lower end of the price range. Note that altering the hem of your dress should be fairly affordable as long as you already have your shoes at the first fitting. Hemming can get expensive if your seamstress repeatedly has to raise and lower the hem because you don't know what shoes you're planning on wearing and the length of your dress consequently keeps changing.

More complex alterations such as adding or removing cups, remodelling the dress, lace or beadwork, will increase the overall alterations costs. As will amendments to a dress with multiple layers or a fuller skirt.

If you are feeling nervous about the ever-increasing factors that you're having to add to your wedding spreadsheet, then you could always send photographs of you in your dress to your seamstress ahead of your first fitting. That way, you will be able to get a rough estimate of costs.

What Happens at Alteration Fittings?

Again, all seamstresses work in different ways, but here is a rough illustration of your alterations process based on three fittings.

First fitting. Here you will meet your seamstress or a member of their team, and they will have a good look at you in your dress! Make sure you are wearing the undies that you plan on wearing to your wedding and *don't forget your shoes!* They will discuss with you any changes they recommend and you can also share any concerns or requests you may have.

The dress is usually (but not always) pinned and your seamstress may ask you to walk around her studio to make sure you aren't tripping on your dress, amid other likely tests.

Second fitting. This is when you can try on your dress now that most, if not all, of the initial work has been completed. Your seamstress will explain the work they have undertaken and check that you are happy with everything.

Please don't kick off at your bridal boutique because your dress is huge on you after you've gone down five dress sizes, thanks to your mad dieting bender in the last year or so.

Third or final fitting. Any further tweaks would have been completed and your beautiful gown should be prepped and ready to go! ARGH!!!!

Please don't forget! It is extremely likely that your dress will need altering. As I mentioned previously, most dresses are Made to Order and your dress will have been ordered in a size that is the most appropriate according to your measurements taken at the time of you placing your order.

Chapter Takeaway

I know I've just given you a hell of a lot of information, so let me summarise all the key info.

Wedding dresses are typically either Made to Order or Made to Measure and it is likely that, once measured, you will fall between two or three dress sizes. Your dress will be ordered in the larger size as it is easier to take a dress in than to let it out.

Two to three fitting appointments with your seamstress should be more than enough, but you must speak up if any part of the dress still doesn't feel secure or comfortable.

And most importantly, don't forget to take your blimmin' shoes to your first fitting!

Chapter 8
Don't Be *That* Bride!

Well-behaved women rarely make history.

No bride wants the reputation of being a Bridezilla. Nor do they want to be *that* bride: the one bride that traumatises a bridal consultant so much that the boutique is still talking about her years later.

So here are my tips on how to avoid being *that* bride.

Sweet Little Darlings

The general consensus is that children and bridal boutiques do not mix. I've had mannequins fall on little girls because they're dicking around in the dresses. I've had champagne glasses smash because of an "amusing" idea for a photo op ("Let's pretend she's drinking champagne!"). And I've even had a potty full of a little darling's wee presented to me with the request "Could you get rid of this for me?".

We completely appreciate that babies need their mothers and can't be left to fend for themselves. But toddlers and older children can't sit still for two hours in a shop full of temptations – nor should we expect them to.

That said, bridal boutiques aren't trying to make your lives difficult (a lot of us our parents ourselves). We completely appreciate that childcare is one of life's endless headaches. So, if you are dealing with a babysitter dilemma, just give your boutique a call and pre-warn them. Please don't do as one bride did and turn up with a toddler, proceed to empty out a sackload of toys into the middle of the fitting area then request a glass of water so the little one could wash her paintbrushes whilst she completed one of her masterpieces. I'm sorry, but in what universe do watercolours and wedding dresses seem like an ideal combination!?

Don't Be Mean!

Not to your bridal stylist, your guests or even the dresses!

You most certainly *are* the most important person in the room. However, that doesn't mean it is okay to have a go at your poor mum because she's not holding the phone at a flattering angle while taking pics of you in your dress. Nor is it okay to bark demands at the poor work-experience girl who's desperately trying to floof your train, pour your Prosecco and tidy dresses. Let's not forget our manners. And whilst we're on that point, please don't be rude about the dresses your stylists are suggesting you try. I've heard brides say, "Urgh, that's hideous!" and, "OMG, this is disgusting! Get it off me!" We get it. You're not going to love every dress you try on, but please be respectful of the fact that someone has taken an extremely long amount of time to painstakingly design and make that gown. Likewise, boutiques fork out tens of thousands of pounds every season to have these dresses in their stores and your insults hit us in the same way they would if you were slagging off our children.

It may not be your dress, but it is someone's.

Be on Time

There's nothing more frustrating than a bride wandering in, Starbucks in hand, 15, 20, 25 minutes late for their appointment, completely oblivious to the amount of mess this makes for the bookings for the rest of that day. Particularly on a Saturday, typically the busiest day for a boutique, when stores are likely to be back to back with bookings. What may seem like an insignificant delay to you will delay every subsequent bride and ultimately mean your stylist can't have her tea until 9pm after she's played catch up. On the flipside, don't get pissy with a boutique if you turn up 20 minutes early for your appointment and the team isn't ready for you. Just arrive at your designated booking time and everyone will be happy.

Be Considerate

If you're unable to attend your appointment, please let the boutique know. Just not turning up, without any notice, is quite simply fucking rude. You wouldn't do that to your hairdresser, so why do it to us?

Don't Tell Fibs

It may sound like a hoot to get your friends together and have one of you pretend you are engaged so that you can have a laugh trying on wedding dresses. But for us bridal boutiques, it's really not fun. It's actually really fucking annoying.

Don't Come in Hungover...

..or let any of your bride tribe come in hungover. They will vomit in our toilets, not tell us, and then leave us to clean it up whilst retching into our jumpers because the smell of sick makes us want to pass out.

Don't Eat a Big Lunch Before Your Appointment...

...and then moan about looking and feeling bloated in every dress you try on like it's our fault because we force-fed that panini down your throat.

And a Couple of Other Little Suggestions

Adhere to Boutique Guidelines

For instance, if a boutique only permits the bride to bring two guests to their appointment, then please only take *two* guests.

Don't turn up with seven friends and then, when the store manager only allows two of those guests to enter the shop, yell appalling obscenities at her through the letterbox.

Don't Rely on Manifestation

Please don't allow a bridal stylist to spend two hours with you finding your dream dress. Don't let her take your measurements, complete all the paperwork and then, when it comes to paying your deposit, inform her that you don't actually have the funds to pay for a wedding dress right now, but the store need not worry as you have *manifested* the money.

Don't Compare Your Wedding to an Act of War...

Your wedding is a hugely important day and I am absolutely not disputing that. But let's be real – any issues that may arise aren't comparable to the war in the Ukraine. So please excuse our stunned silence when you ask us what our "plan" is if disaster strikes and the factory where your dress is being made gets bombed. Likewise if, let's say, a mother calls us to query any potential delays with the production of her daughter's Ukraine-produced wedding dress. Please know that our apologies are very sincere when we inform her that we have been unable to make any direct contact with a designer living directly in a war zone.

I do also hope that the totally fictional aforementioned mother would simply accept the apology, instead of screaming down the phone, "I know there's a war going on, but you NEED to understand things from my perspective. This is *my daughter's wedding dress!*"

...Or a Global Pandemic...

It is unlikely that any bridal boutique will have the gravitas or power to lift restrictions in a national lockdown situation. Nor is it likely that the store owner will have a direct line of contact with the sitting Prime Minister to enable them to obtain an approximate date as to when these restrictions will be relaxed. So when you are informed of this unfortunate information, please don't scream, "It's *my* day. I DESERVE MY MOMENT!" at the boutique team member.

...Or Childbirth

If a bridal boutique owner provides you with her personal mobile phone number because she is desperately trying to lessen the impact of her leaving the business momentarily to give birth to another human being, it is unlikely that she is happy for you to call her a day or so after the birth. I also suspect that she probably wasn't expecting you or your mother to text her at 4am two weeks after the birth, exclaiming "I know you've just had a baby..." and then demand that the owner (along with her newborn, her milky udders and her plethora of stitches) attend her alteration's appointment the following day.

Obviously, none of you would ever behave in this way, would you!? No, of course not!

"Do NOT Come Near Me With That Steamer!"

After all the hard work you've put into finding your dream wedding dress, I'm not going to let it all go to shit by having you walk down the aisle in a creased gown with foundation smeared round the neckline. So here are some final tips and tricks to make sure your dress remains as flawless as you are....

Let her breathe

Once you get your dress to where it needs to be, get it out of the garment bag and let it settle. Hang it as high as you can (a door frame, a curtain rail, a very tall man...) and away from direct sunlight, so that any creases that may have developed en route can drop out.

Hang your dress by the hanging ribbons (NOT the straps as they will stretch), but make sure you have a pair of scissors handy so that you can cut the ribbons off when you put the dress on. The last thing you want is for those little buggers to creep out from your armpits as you walk down the aisle.

Let your dress relax!

If there are any stubborn creases, do not – I repeat, DO NOT – let a well-meaning member of your wedding party come at you with a steamer. Steaming a wedding dress correctly really is an art. And if it's not done properly your gown will be covered in water marks before you can say "Pre-Nup!"

All you need to do is hang your dress in the bathroom and turn on the heat! Close the doors and the windows, run a bath or a shower and any crinkles will drop out within minutes.

That said, if you *really* feel the need to steam your dress, then please have a chat with your bridal boutique beforehand and they can advise you of all the best tips and techniques to prevent any horrific watermarks on the front of your dress.

Don't marinate

I know we all plan to waft down the aisle in a cloud of No. 5, but please be careful with your body creams and perfumes. Apply any body creams immediately after you've had a bath or shower and preferably a few hours before you plan to put your dress on. This prevents any greasy marks from transferring onto the fabric. The same applies to fragrance – Spritz, bathe, marinate – whichever works for you. Then let the scent dry before putting your dress on; otherwise, you'll get pissy yellow stains on your dress. If you can bring yourself just to "kiss" your pulse points (wrists, inside your elbows etc) with perfume, then that's even better. But you're a stronger woman than I am. I like the strength of my fragrance to be so strong that it makes people's eyes water.

Socks

....and bras need to be left in the drawer... no matter how cosy they are. Otherwise, you'll be walking down the aisle with corrugated shins and dented shoulders. Correct me if I'm wrong, but I don't think that's the look you're going for.

Buttons

If your dress has 235,374,848 buttons, then make sure you pack a crochet hook as it's the ideal tool to grab the loops and hook them over the buttons without breaking a nail or getting a thumb cramp. If you can't get your hands on a crochet hook, then a hairpin is a good alternative.

Step in

Ideally, you will be stepping *into* your dress. But if for any reason it needs to go on over your head, then drape a *silk* scarf over your head before putting it on. That should protect your hair and stop you from getting makeup on the dress.

Have a sausage sandwich

...Or whatever your choice of breakfast may be. Believe me, this is *so* important. My bridesmaids and I didn't allow time for this when I had my first wedding, and we were all pretty pissed by the time we needed to leave for the church. One of my bridesmaids even heckled the vicar! (No names mentioned…Victoria.)

Pack an emergency kit

Paracetamol, antihistamines, plasters, scissors, mini sewing kit, safety pins, tampons, stain remover, talc (it's a lifesaver if, like me, you suffer from sweaty, chaffing thighs), baby wipes, white chalk (perfect for covering any marks that suddenly appear on your dress), nail file, mints, shotgun….

Conclusion

May all your marriage ups and downs only happen in the bedroom.

Congrats, Bridey! You did it! You've made it to the end of this incredibly hilarious (if I do say so myself), sometimes brutal, no-holds-barred guide to wedding dress shopping. I knew you could do it and never doubted you for a second.

By now, you should have an arsenal filled with newly found knowledge, confidence and a fair few belly laughs to carry you through this unforgettable journey. Remember, this experience isn't just about finding your dream dress, it's about celebrating who you are as an individual.

As you step into that final fitting, take a moment to reflect on all the madness you have navigated. From the wild card dresses that made you question everything to the ridiculous comments and advice (but I'm sure it was also well-meaning…I think…) from your family and friends, each part of this journey is now a story that you can pop into your memory bank. Embrace it all – the laughter, the stress and the occasional need to hide in the fitting room and silently scream "Fuuuuuuuuuccccck!"

Here are a few final reminders. Pop them on some Post-its and stick them on the bathroom mirror to look at whenever you need reminding of your "mission": to find a wedding dress that makes you look and feel like a fucking goddess.

Be yourself. Your wedding dress should reflect your unique personality and style. Don't let anyone pressure you into wearing a gown that *they* want you to wear (just so they can tell everyone, "Oh yeah, it was me who found the wedding dress. I'm *such* an amazing person"). And don't conform to anyone else's vision of what a wedding dress or you as a bride "should" look like.

Trust your instincts. Listen to your gut when choosing your dress. Only you know what makes you feel beautiful.

There will *always* be more dresses. There will also always be more fiancés, but we have to stop looking and eventually commit.

Expect the unexpected. Be open to surprises. You might fall in love with a style you never even considered before, so don't limit yourself.

If you have no intention of ordering your dress…don't start shopping, because you *will* find The One.

Just because neither you nor your entourage are crying…doesn't mean you haven't found the perfect dress.

If you fall in love with a dress you tried on at your very first bridal appointment…go ahead and order it.

If you need to sleep on it, if you can honestly walk away from your dream dress, then chances are it's not "The One."

Don't ever let anyone tell you that a dress you love "isn't a proper wedding dress."

So, as you gear up for your big day, remember that the best accessory you can wear with your wedding dress is joy (don't roll your eyes at me, you know it's true). But it's also a good idea to keep this little guide close at hand. If anything, it will remind you to block out all the background noise and not take anyone's shit.

I hope you have the *best* wedding. You're going to have such an amazing day and I'm actually really jealous. I'm so jealous, in fact, that I may need to go and find husband number three…

What's Next?

It isn't over yet, Bridey! While you've got your complete guide in this book, I'd love for you to come check out Tilly Trotter's Brides. It doesn't matter if you're not in the UK as you can pop by our website anytime at https://tillytrottersbrides.co.uk/about-us/the-experience.

You can also drop us a line on our Instagram, where we love to celebrate our gorgeous brides and their gorgeous dresses. Keep in touch at https://instagram.com/tilly_trotters_brides.

Glossary of Weird Bridal Language That Often Makes No Sense

Appliqué – An additional, decorative piece of fabric (usually lace or beadwork) that is sewn onto your wedding dress.

A-line – A shape of a wedding dress, so called because it resembles the letter "A."

Alterations – The changes made to your dress by a seamstress to make it fit perfectly to your body.

Asymmetric – Also known as "one-shoulder". This is a lovely, modest neckline, but should be avoided if you feel you have broader arms, as it can cut you off at the widest part.

Ballgown – A traditional "princess" style of wedding dress that has a fitted bodice and a fuller, more dramatic skirt.

Basque – The bodice part of a wedding dress that sits just below the waistline and has a subtle "V" shape.

Bell sleeve – A voluminous sleeve that's large and flowing and usually fitted at the wrist.

Black Tie – A more formal dress code which requires men to wear a tuxedo and women to wear a formal cocktail dress or floor-length gown.

Boning – The structural part of a wedding dress bodice that helps it to stay up.

Bustle – A clever little addition! Your seamstress will sew a button or some kind of hook into the train of your dress so that you can fasten it up and out of the way in the evening, meaning you can bust those moves on the dance floor without your dress getting in the way.

Bardot – A neckline that sits just off the shoulders to show the top of the arms. This is a flattering cut that's great for showing off necklaces, but, like asymmetric necklines, you should avoid these if you feel you have broader arms, as it can cut you off at the widest part.

Bateau or boat – A neckline that is cut from shoulder to shoulder, straight across the collarbone.

Birdcage – The name given to a veil that is fixed in the hair and falls to just below the cheeks or no further than the jawline.

Cap sleeve – A short sleeve that covers the top of your arm.

Cathedral – The name given to a veil that generally extends past the train of a wedding dress.

Column – A slim-cut dress that falls straight down to the floor.

Crepe – Not the pancake. A thinner fabric with an almost matte effect to it. It is not as "shiny" as Mikado.

Chiffon – Very soft, floaty silk.

Drop waist – A dress shape where the waist seam falls below the natural waistline to the mid-hip.

Darts – Small triangular seams that are added to your dress to help it fit more snuggly to your curves.

Empire or empire-line – A high waistline that starts under the bust area.

Fishtail – A dress shape that is fitted all the way down the body and flares out at the knee.

Fit and flare – See "Fishtail." Can also be more of a subtle flare at the knee compared to a fishtail.

Hem – The finished edge of a fabric. When we refer to the hem of your dress, we're usually talking about the bottom of the skirt.

Halterneck – A dress with no sleeves that usually fastens at the back of the neck, with deep cut armholes showing off the shoulders and top of the arms.

Illusion – A flesh-coloured piece of tulle (mesh) that is added to a dress to give the appearance of less coverage than there actually is. You will tend to find an illusion section added to the bodice of a dress, for example, to make a plunge look less "plungey."

Made to Measure – A custom wedding gown that is made to your exact body measurements. It is an existing design that is then made to fit your body shape and not a *bespoke* design made to your specifications.

Made to Order – A dress that is made to a standard dress size and is then altered to fit you perfectly by a seamstress.

Mermaid – See "Fit and Flare."

Mikado - A heavier, more structural fabric used in dresses. Mikado can have a slight sheen or a matte diagonal weave and is typically shinier than crepe, but more subtle than satin.

Overskirt – An additional skirt that can be worn over the top of a fitted dress to add more volume and drama. This is also a great way of creating two different looks for your day.

Plunge – A deep "V" neckline that starts from the shoulders and comes to meet anywhere from the cleavage to the belly button!

Pleats – Wide folds in the fabric.

Ruching – The term used to describe the gathering or bunching together of fabric. Like pleats but with a softer effect.

Satin - A lighter fabric compared to Mikado, with a more lustrous sheen.

Seamstress – The magician who alters your dress to make it fit perfectly to your body.

Sheath – See "Column."

Split-size – A term used when your measurements fall between two or three different sizes. For example, your bust and waist measurements correspond to a size 12, but your hip measurement matches a 14. You are consequently *split-size*...split between a size 12 and size 14.

Sweetheart – A neckline that is shaped like the top of a heart across the bust.

Sample – The name given to the dresses that you try in a bridal boutique. A bit like a "display model" in a car showroom!

Sample Sale – A special event where brides can purchase shop sample dresses at a discounted price. These dresses have typically been tried on by other brides and may show minor signs of wear, but they offer a great opportunity to find a high-quality gown at a discount. It is likely that there will only be one of each style of dress available, as boutiques tend to only hold one dress in one size.

Silhouette – Another name for wedding dress *shape*.

Siân – The author of the best bridal book you will ever read.

Taffeta – A "crisp" fabric, usually from silk.

Train – The long bit at the back of the dress that trails behind you when you walk.

Trunkshow – If a store is hosting a trunkshow, it means they will have the newest collection of one specific designer in store, usually for a very limited period of time. It is rare that a boutique will stock an entire collection of any designer so it's always a great opportunity to book an appointment at a trunkshow event if one comes up in your area, particularly if it involves a collection from a designer you love.

Tulle – A soft, net type of fabric that is used in dresses, sometimes in the overall design, sometimes just in the skirt and sometimes in a flesh colour as an illusion panel.

Tilly Trotter's Brides – The best bridal boutique in the UK.

Acknowledgements

This book would 10,000% not have been possible without the support and immense patience of my writing mentor Angela Haynes-Ranger. Not only has she guided me through this whole process, but she hasn't once called me out when I've given her excuses for not meeting deadlines, she's continually laughed at my stupid humour and she's attempted to converse with my dogs over our Zoom calls. Thank you for everything.

Eternal thanks go to Christine Wilke for her exquisite illustrations. You made this book beautiful and I honestly cannot thank you enough.

And to my incredible friend Charlie Brear for taking the time to write such a beautiful foreword...You're an inspiration.

Love and thanks to my family, Dad and Lyn, Sue and Fi...and my little piglet Knox!

To my friends Leanne and Victoria – who have merchandised windows, designed logos and done more than their fair share of shifts at Tilly's. And not forgetting Karen, Vicki, Joyce, Caroline, Julie, Becci, Rachael, Nicky, Shannon, Victoria E., Alice, Kerry, my little Freya and of course, Smiles. Each and every one of you has supported me in some way throughout the last 10 years of Tilly's and I can't thank you enough. You mean the world to me.

Laura - Tilly's would quite simply not exist if it wasn't for your love and dedication. You are the heart and soul of the boutique, and I am so blessed to have you in my life and to be able to call you a friend.

Omitz, thank you for always helping me out when I'm neck-deep in shit, getting loans for me to buy stock, covering the shop when I have no staff – the list is endless. Most importantly, thank you for being such a reliable Womble, and for always taking an excessive amount of unwanted coat hangers and empty plastic wallets off my hands. I love you!

Moony, my spiritual sister, thank you for being the most amazing best friend for nearly 30 years. You're always my biggest cheerleader and your unwavering faith in me and everything I do never fails to blow me away. I'm so grateful to the universe for bringing you into my life.

Adam, my incredible husband, thank you for your unconditional love and support. A day doesn't go by that you don't make me happy, and for that, I will be eternally grateful. I will love you forever.

Hector, my little prince! You are my best friend and my greatest achievement. I am so proud to be your Mummy. I love you to infinity, Sausage.

To the dogs DeeDee, Margot (Tippy), Claude, Clive and Renee, thank you for your unconditional love and for continuously shitting on the carpet.

And finally, to Mum. I wish you were still alive to read this book. I think you would have enjoyed it. At least I can be happy knowing you would be proud of my grammar, spelling and punctuation. (You wouldn't have been as impressed with all the swear words, but we'll ignore that.)

Printed in Great Britain
by Amazon